>

GREATER
DEVOTIONAL

A 40-DAY EXPERIENCE
TO IGNITE GOD'S VISION FOR YOUR LIFE

>

GREATER
DEVOTIONAL

NEW YORK TIMES BEST-SELLING AUTHOR
STEVEN FURTICK
with ERIC STANFORD

MULTNOMAH
BOOKS

GREATER DEVOTIONAL
PUBLISHED BY MULTNOMAH BOOKS
12265 Oracle Boulevard, Suite 200
Colorado Springs, Colorado 80921

All Scripture quotations, unless otherwise indicated, are taken from the Holy Bible, New International Version®, NIV®. Copyright © 1973, 1978, 1984, 2011 by Biblica Inc.™ Used by permission of Zondervan. All rights reserved worldwide. www.zondervan.com. Scripture quotations marked (ESV) are taken from The Holy Bible, English Standard Version, copyright © 2001 by Crossway Bibles, a division of Good News Publishers. Used by permission. All rights reserved. Scripture quotations marked (NKJV) are taken from the New King James Version®. Copyright © 1982 by Thomas Nelson Inc. Used by permission. All rights reserved.

Hardcover ISBN 978-1-60142-525-6
eBook ISBN 978-1-60142-526-3

Cover design by Ryan Hollingsworth

Published in the United States by WaterBrook Multnomah, an imprint of the Crown Publishing Group, a division of Random House LLC, New York, a Penguin Random House Company.

MULTNOMAH and its mountain colophon are registered trademarks of Random House LLC.

Library of Congress Cataloging-in-Publication Data
Furtick, Steven.
    Greater devotional : a 40-day experience to ignite God's vision for your life / Steven Furtick, New York Times best-selling author, with Eric Stanford. — First Edition.
        pages cm
    ISBN 978-1-60142-525-6 — ISBN 978-1-60142-526-3 (electronic) 1. Christian life—Biblical teaching. I. Title.
    BS680.C47F87 2014
    242'.4—dc23

                                                        2014019599

Printed in the United States of America
2014—First Edition

10 9 8 7 6 5 4 3 2 1

SPECIAL SALES
Most WaterBrook Multnomah books are available at special quantity discounts when purchased in bulk by corporations, organizations, and special-interest groups. Custom imprinting or excerpting can also be done to fit special needs. For information, please e-mail SpecialMarkets@WaterBrookMultnomah.com or call 1-800-603-7051.

Meant for More

Lately it seems like I'm meeting more and more believers who are unsatisfied with the kind of Christians they're becoming and the version of the Christian life they're experiencing. These aren't bad people. They aren't gangbangers and ungodly pagans. If they were, their discontent would make more sense.

The thing is, most believers aren't in imminent danger of ruining their lives. They're facing a danger that's far greater: *wasting them*. I worry about that risk for myself, and maybe you're the same way.

We've had some big dreams about what God might want for our lives. But so many of us are stuck in the starting blocks. Or are dragging along at the back of the pack.

We know we were meant for more. Yet we end up settling for less.

We're frustrated about where we are. But we're confused about how to move forward.

If this is where you are, the *Greater Devotional* is for you.

For the next forty days, we'll learn to spend time with God and His Word to find out how He wants to expand our world. The devotionals are based on some key ideas I talk about in my book *Greater*. Much of the material is brand-new to print, and here the focus is on the spiritual journey necessary to get from "good enough" to "greater." We'll be looking at a lot of events in the life of the prophet Elisha, but we'll also be mining other rich texts from all over the Bible.

These devotionals are not primarily meant to give you a cozy feeling or make you satisfied because you've met a spiritual requirement. They are meant to yank you from the mediocrity you may have grown accustomed to and set you on the course to a greater destiny.

The call to be greater is the call to walk with God Himself. And, in fact, I believe any lasting transformation flows from divine revelation. More can be accomplished in a half hour of prayer, worship, and listening to the voice of the Holy Spirit than in a month of strategizing on our own.

I can trace my most frustrating seasons to a deficiency of time I allocated to my most important task: seeking the wisdom of the Lord. And, conversely, I can trace the genesis of many of the most important changes in my life, my family, and my church to specific moments I spent in the presence of God. That's why I believe you have every reason to expect amazing things to happen as you spend time with God for the next forty days.

Dream big.

Start small.

Ignite God's vision for your life, starting today.

The Muck of Mediocrity

Very truly I tell you, whoever believes in me will do the works I have been doing, and they will do even greater things than these, because I am going to the Father.

—JOHN 14:12

Today's Bible reading: John 14:1–14

For most of us, the experience of our daily lives is a far cry from the greater works Jesus talked about in John 14:12. We know instinctively, even if we can't articulate it exactly, that something isn't squaring up. There's a huge gap between what God said in His Word and the results we see in our lives.

It's like we've been lulled into comfortable complacency. Then we wake up one day to find ourselves stuck in miserable mediocrity. So we tuck away any dreams and notions of the great things we'd like to do for God.

After all, we're doing good. Good enough. It kind of sucks. But it's all we know.

If that's where you are today, I need to share a strong word of warning with you.

You can't keep living like this. It's not fine for you to settle for going every day to a job you'd prefer to quit, doing decent work, being a pretty good person compared to your neighbor, paying your bills on time, and sporadically reading the Bible as though it's your guide to the great things God did in other people's lives in the past.

🔁 RT We can be so much better than we've become, because God is so much greater than we're allowing Him to be through us. #GreaterBook

---

Baseline living is not okay. Not for a believer in Jesus. There's a price to pay for Christian complacency. If you keep living on this level, your heart is going to shrivel. It might already be shriveling. Your dreams are going to die. They may already be on life support. Will you look up one day and be overwhelmed by the stack of regrets staring back at you? The frustration that's simmering on the back burner right now might boil over one day, and you'll be bitter about the opportunities you missed. Opportunities to be used by God, to touch lives, to get outside yourself and be a part of something greater. I know it's not easy. But don't tell me it's not possible. Jesus Himself said it was.

The fact is, we can be so much better than we've become, because God is so much greater than we're allowing Him to be through us. That's why, for forty days, we're asking God to show us His picture of the greater life and help us go after it. Start today by telling yourself you don't have to stay stuck in the muck of mediocrity. Open your spirit up to the possibility of something greater. Open it up to Jesus Himself.

PRAYER FOCUS: Ask God to ignite in you a vision of the different life He wants you to live. Commit to a lifestyle of listening for His voice.

Behind the Scenes

The LORD said to [Elijah],..."Anoint Elisha son
of Shaphat from Abel Meholah to succeed you as
prophet."

—1 KINGS 19:15–16

Today's Bible reading: 1 Kings 19:15–21

In many of these devotionals, we're going to be using the biblical character Elisha as a model of what a greater life can be like. For Elisha, it all started on an ordinary day—just like today probably is for you. The predictable beat of his ordinary life was interrupted and everything changed.

The interruption didn't happen the way most of us would think it should. God's interruptions rarely do. Elisha didn't go to a career fair or meet with a life coach to talk about some new possibilities. He wasn't looking for a different kind of life at all. And get this—Elisha wasn't praying. Instead, he was doing the best he could with the life he assumed he'd been handed. He was plowing a field behind a bunch of oxen's rears.

But hundreds of miles away, God had been talking about Elisha behind his back. The gist of the conversation was that He had something greater for him. A divine calling beyond his imagination. He was to become the successor to the most famous prophet in Israel's history: Elijah.

Elisha didn't know it yet, but Elijah was already in his neighborhood, with plans to toss his mantle over the plowman's shoulders. After that encounter, nothing would be the same. The presence of Elijah, in what seemed to be an ordinary situation, would thrust Elisha's life in an extraordinary new direction.

RT Just because you haven't heard God call your name doesn't mean He's not orchestrating great things for you. #GreaterBook

---

I've experienced such sudden opportunities in my life, unexpected invitations from God to do something greater. I believe you will too.

God is often working behind the scenes of your life, orchestrating His destiny for you even though you don't have a clue about what He's up to. He wants to pull you out of the muck of mediocrity. Just because you haven't heard God call your name or tell you specifically what to do with your life, that doesn't mean He's not orchestrating great things for you.

I guess you could say God likes to sneak up on you.

You're marching along to the beat of the ordinary, and then one day the ordinary is interrupted by a calling. That calling can change everything if you know how to discern it.

So that makes me ask…

Do you have enough faith to believe God is preparing something greater for you right now?

While you are doing your best in your life as it exists, are you looking for invitations to do the new things God has in store for you?

Most important…

Elisha "ran after Elijah," the story tells us (verse 20). Are you ready to run after God's greater calling for you?

PRAYER FOCUS: Ask for faith to believe that God is preparing you for greater things—and for the ability to recognize His plans when He reveals them to you.

I Give Up

Therefore, I urge you, brothers and sisters, in view of God's mercy, to offer your bodies as a living sacrifice, holy and pleasing to God—this is your true and proper worship. Do not conform to the pattern of this world, but be transformed by the renewing of your mind. Then you will be able to test and approve what God's will is—his good, pleasing and perfect will.

—Romans 12:1–2

Today's Bible reading: Romans 11:33–12:2

I love the final verses in Romans 11. "Oh, the depth of the riches of the wisdom and knowledge of God!... To him be the glory forever!" What believer wouldn't agree with that and say amen along with Paul?

But what's interesting to me is what happens when we get into Romans 12. Here's where we discover our proper response to the greatness of God: surrender. We're to climb up on the altar as a sacrifice. We're to let God remold us completely.

The first thing Elisha did when God called him to become Elijah's successor was to burn his plows and use the resulting fire to cook his animals (1 Kings 19:21). Continuing his old trade would have been conforming to the pattern of this world. Not because there's anything intrinsically wrong with plowing with oxen, but because God was specifically calling him into something different. So Elisha made a sharp break with the past. He was transformed to follow God's good, pleasing, and perfect will for him in the greater life of a prophet.

The first thing God is calling you to, in order to fulfill a greater purpose in your life, is surrender. We must acknowledge how great God is, how He surpasses everything else in the world that we could aim for or aspire to, and how we'll never be great on our own.

When Jesus called us to do greater things in John 14:12, He wasn't calling us to be greater *than* Him. He was calling us to be greater *through* Him by using His power living inside us so we can do greater things for His glory. So before you go on to do greater things, you have to deal with the question, is my heart surrendered to God?

RT The first thing God is calling you to, in order to fulfill a greater purpose in your life, is surrender. #GreaterBook

---

Is there an area in your life today where you feel like you need to burn your plow, that connection to a part of your life you haven't given completely over to God? Before God can begin to make something greater out of your life, before you can step into the life you're wanting, you've got to give Him all of the life you have, because He gave it to you to begin with.

That's why Ephesians 3:20 says that God "is able to do immeasurably more than all we ask or imagine, according to his power that is at work within us." He is great, and He wants greater things for us than we can imagine for ourselves. So when you take a posture of surrender, you say, "God, here it is. You're the producer. Tell me what part to play. You're my leader. Tell me where to go. You're the creator and commander of my life. I'm completely submitted to You."

God will call different people to do different things. But it's always something greater than our human minds alone could ever conceive. And it always starts with surrender.

PRAYER FOCUS: Will you burn your plow? Will you offer yourself as a living sacrifice? Express your surrender to God. Be as specific about the "plow" as you possibly can.

Spiritual Hearing Test

As the rain and the snow
come down from heaven,
and do not return to it
without watering the earth
and making it bud and flourish,
so that it yields seed for the sower and bread
for the eater,
so is my word that goes out from my mouth:
It will not return to me empty,
but will accomplish what I desire
and achieve the purpose for which I sent it.

—Isaiah 55:10–11

Today's Bible reading: Isaiah 55:6–13

A few years ago I had a crazy ringing in my ears. I was afraid I was losing my hearing because of all the loud rock music I played when I was growing up. The doctor did some tests, and it turned out I had lost a little hearing at certain frequencies. But surprisingly, he said something that encouraged me.

"The ringing in your ears is a good thing," he told me. "It

might be annoying, but it's proof that you still have hearing left. When the ringing goes away, that means that your hearing has completely died."

Do you have a spiritual ringing in the ears? Is God trying to tell you something? If you're feeling the vibrations of the sound of God speaking to you, even if you can't clearly decode it yet, it means your ability and desire to hear from Him is still intact. And even if you have lost some of your sensitivity to God's voice, you can get your spiritual hearing back.

As Hebrews 3:7–8 says, "Today, if you hear his voice, do not harden your hearts." Listen. And respond in obedience.

RT When was the last time God prompted you to take a bold risk for Him and you took Him up on it? #GreaterBook

---

Let's make up our minds right now to accept God's ways, which are higher than our ways, and His thoughts, which are higher than our thoughts. Let's say, "God, I'm open to Your greater plan for my life, whatever that may be."

So just as my doctor made me listen to certain sounds to see if I could detect them, let me give you a spiritual hearing test.

- When was the last time God told you to encourage somebody and you did it?
- When was the last time God showed you a trouble spot in a relationship with somebody, and you went to that person and tried to make the relationship right?

- When was the last time God showed you something in your life that wasn't necessarily bad but wasn't exactly best, and you stopped it just because He said so?
- When was the last time God gave you an opportunity to give sacrificially and you did it cheerfully?
- When was the last time God told you to take a bold risk for Him and you took Him up on it?

The key to the greater life is developing a strong sense of spiritual hearing. Then you can discern how God is calling you, not only to be His child, but also to follow Him and be His disciple.

PRAYER FOCUS: Ask God to help you clear away any obstructions to your spiritual hearing so you can detect every call to greater things when it comes.

Cloudy with a Chance of Revelation

When Moses went up on the mountain, the cloud covered it, and the glory of the LORD settled on Mount Sinai. For six days the cloud covered the mountain, and on the seventh day the LORD called to Moses from within the cloud.

—EXODUS 24:15–16

Today's Bible reading: Exodus 24

I think we have some major misconceptions when it comes to knowing God's will. We often assume it's a streamlined, expedient process. You pray, and immediately you know what you're supposed to do. You fast, and the answer you're looking for magically comes before the second skipped meal. You open your Bible, and your sight lands on a random verse in Colossians that tells you what decision to make.

Sometimes that happens. But not usually. Usually it's more like what Moses experienced on the mountain.

Moses was at Mount Sinai to meet with the Lord and receive

directions and the Law for the people. He wanted to know the will of God. God wanted him to know it even more. But then Moses just sat there. God eventually spoke to him, but it was only after Moses had waited for six days in cloudy silence.

That should be encouraging to those of us who still don't know God's will for a particular situation or our life in general, and we think we never will. How can you make use of that spiritual gift you've sensed within yourself but never really practiced? Has the time come to make the leap into that business venture you've had in mind? Should you get your degree? Move? Marry? Have kids? Stop having kids?

The will of God often takes time to determine. Cloudy conditions usually come before clear commands. Sometimes God speaks to us immediately and clearly, as He did when Elijah threw his cloak over Elisha's shoulders. When He does, we should be thankful for those times and act immediately and boldly. But usually, we're going to spend days, months, maybe even years in the clouds before we hear anything.

RT Cloudy conditions usually come before clear commands. #GreaterBook

---

If that's you right now, don't head back down the mountain just yet. God has a clear direction coming for you. And remember, you're not alone. God's silence is not equivalent to God's absence. The divine glory was on the mountain with Moses every one of those six days before Moses heard anything. Time spent in worship as you wait on God is never wasted. But as you wait, obey the will of God that you already know. Waiting on God is an active pursuit, not a passive attitude.

God is going to speak to you. He wants you to know His will for your life more than you want to know His will for your life. But He will reveal it on His timetable, according to His purpose.

PRAYER FOCUS: Ask God for patience and persistence as you wait for His will to emerge from the fog.

Perfect for You

Father, if you are willing, take this cup from me;
yet not my will, but yours be done.

—LUKE 22:42

Today's Bible reading: Luke 22:39–46

Every true believer desires to be in God's will. Sometimes we even talk about wanting to be in the "perfect will" of God. But God's perfect will might not look like we think it should.

Perhaps we should clear up what we mean by "perfect." Otherwise, we could miss out on God's will altogether in our pursuit of greater, because we'll be too busy chasing our own ideas.

Our idea of perfect is something that seems perfect *to* us. What seems like a perfect day *to* you might mean everything is going the way you think it should go. What seems like a perfect marriage *to* you might be one that's easy and stress free. What seems like a perfect job *to* you might be one where you're high on the leadership pyramid and banking loads of cash.

All of these scenarios can be blessings from God, and it's fine to pray about these kinds of things. Our heavenly Father loves to give good and perfect gifts. But sometimes, what God decides is perfect *for* us will look much different than what seems perfect *to* us. And ultimately, we must learn to approach every situation believing that what is perfect *to God* is perfect *for us*. God's will for you is to become everything He dreamed you to be so that you might glorify Him the way He deserves to be glorified. And that doesn't necessarily happen through easy circumstances or perfect conditions.

God's will doesn't have to seem perfect *to* you to be perfect *for* you.

If you need proof of this, take a glance at the Bible.

God's will for Job didn't seem perfect to Job. He lost everything. But it accomplished a perfecting work *for* him and within him. It brought him to a whole new level of faith and positioned him for a greater blessing later in his life.

RT God's will doesn't have to seem perfect *to* you to be perfect *for* you. #GreaterBook

---

God's will for Joseph didn't seem perfect to him. He landed in slavery and prison for over a decade. But it turned out to be perfect for him. Through him, God saved his family and an entire nation.

God's will for Paul probably didn't seem perfect to a lot of people. Few men have ever suffered so much for the gospel. But, as history attests, it was perfect for him. Few men have ever spread the gospel so widely in their lifetime.

God's will for Jesus didn't seem perfect to His disciples. In the

Garden of Gethsemane, He wasn't even sure He wanted it. But it was perfect for Him. He defeated sin on the cross and then conquered death in the Resurrection. And thereby provided His perfect salvation to the whole world.

God's will for you might not always seem perfect to you. But trust me, His will is perfect for you.

The job you hate right now might not seem perfect to you. But through it, maybe God is perfectly developing your character, patience, and faithfulness.

That loss of relationship you just went through might not seem like God's perfect will to you. But the relationship God is clearing space for, and has been preparing you for your entire life, is perfect for you.

The disease you're battling right now might not seem perfect to you. But God could use your pain as a platform for the gospel to reach countless people. And He's putting you in the perfect position to comfort others.

That doesn't make it easy. But it does make it meaningful. Purposeful. Worth it.

And ultimately, perfect.

After all, God's greatest goal isn't to give His people perfect situations but to perfect His people for greater works of service.

PRAYER FOCUS: Pray the way Jesus did in the garden: *God, I'm willing to trade in my will for Yours. Every time. No matter what. Knowing it's for the best.*

The Lifetime of an Opportunity

"The time has come," [John] said. "The kingdom of God has come near."

—MARK 1:15

Today's Bible reading: Mark 1:14–20

I wish I could take credit for this line, but it comes from Leonard Ravenhill, an evangelist of the twentieth century: "The opportunity of a lifetime must be seized in the lifetime of the opportunity."

Think about that...

Every opportunity has an expiration date. Exceptional people, churches, and businesses possess the agility to move at the speed of God. This usually means merging into oncoming traffic at breakneck speed. But we've got to make the decision to do it while we have the chance.

A lot of people I know are more fearful of making a wrong move than of making no move at all. But I'm learning that if I sit at the intersection after God has given me a green light, He'll only honk a few times before the opportunity passes me by in the other lane. That doesn't mean God will stop loving me or stop using me. It just means that this particular opportunity is gone. Forever.

If you are currently looking at a great, godly, risky opportunity, consider this: the cost of missing out can be greater than the cost of messing up.

The opportunity of a lifetime must be seized in the lifetime of the opportunity. That's why the Bible refers to *kairos* time, which is different from regular *chronos* time, or clock time. Kairos time is *the appointed time* in the purpose of God. It is *the fullness of time, the right time for a thing, the opportune moment* to be seized.

"The time has come," John the Baptist said in announcing the appearance of the Messiah (Mark 1:15). Jesus had come at just the right time in history—His own kairos window of opportunity.

RT The opportunity of a lifetime must be seized in the lifetime of the opportunity. #GreaterBook

---

Jesus's followers had, and still have, kairos moments too.

When Jesus called Peter and Andrew to follow Him, "at once" they dropped their nets and went with Him (Mark 1:18). Shortly after, James and John left their boat to join Jesus's crew (verse 20). The opportunity of a lifetime had come to them, and they seized it.

Others have had similar moments and have not responded so well. The rich young ruler was another one who heard the "Follow me" call from Jesus's lips. But unlike the Galilean fishermen, he choked because the cost was higher than he was willing to pay (Luke 18:18–25).

If Jesus is calling you to something, don't wait to obey.

"Be very careful...how you live—not as unwise but as wise," says Paul, "making the most of every opportunity" (Ephesians 5:15–16).

Today's excuse could be tomorrow's regret dressed in disguise.

PRAYER FOCUS: Ask God to help you overcome any hesitation or procrastination you may have about following His call in your life.

Doing the Details

The LORD had said to Abram, "Go from your country, your people and your father's household to the land I will show you."

—GENESIS 12:1

Today's Bible reading: Genesis 12:1–5

Have you ever heard people say, "I don't do details"? They presumably mean by this that they consider themselves big-picture people and don't like to get bogged down in the minutia.

In His own way God doesn't do details either. I'm not saying He doesn't care about the details—Jesus said He has numbered the hairs of your head and is aware of every sparrow that falls to the ground (see Luke 12:6–7). I can't imagine a more meticulous way of managing the universe than that. My point is that, while God is detail oriented, He doesn't handle details or communicate them in the way most of us would prefer. He doesn't feel obliged to walk us through every contingency or provide us with every possible kind of warranty. He simply tells us to trust Him with the outcome, inviting us to act in faith and obedience.

When God says He has something greater to do in your life,

He does not necessarily tell you how He is going to do it, only *that* He is going to do it. And it can be frustrating to follow a God like that.

God's directions can, in fact, seem painfully vague and incomplete. When He told Abraham, "Go…to the land I will show you," He abruptly stopped talking. He didn't give him a road map. He didn't give him a detailed life plan. God didn't give Abraham a GPS. Only a directive: "Abraham—just go." He simply issued the command and expected obedience.

I know that, if you are a pragmatic person, the idea that God will often direct you in this way might make you shudder. But God wasn't being cruel to Abraham, and He's not being cruel to you. There's a good reason He doesn't feel the need to give you a navigational system. It's because He is offering to *be* your navigational system. Which one would you rather have: God's guidance as a commodity or God Himself as your guide?

RT God is more interested in your full obedience than in your full understanding. #GreaterBook

---

He will be faithful to His end of the bargain. He'll do the *showing* as you do the *going*. You can't think too far ahead about where you'll end up. You can only go where He tells you to go today.

When you wake up the next morning, He'll show you where to go tomorrow.

The day after that, He'll show you where to go that day.

And the day after that. And the next day. And the next day.

Moment by moment.

So don't worry. God has every detail of your path to a greater life covered. He just doesn't need you to know these details first to follow Him faithfully. Ultimately, He's more interested in your full obedience than in your full understanding.

PRAYER FOCUS: Ask God to show you the right direction for the next stage of your journey—and to help you accept that as enough information for now.

Double Portion

*Elijah said to Elisha, "Tell me, what can I do for you
before I am taken from you?"*

*"Let me inherit a double portion of your spirit,"
Elisha replied.*

—2 Kings 2:9

Today's Bible reading: 2 Kings 2:1–12

I hope, nine days into this experience, you're feeling excited and
expectant, already seeing some major changes in your life. But let's
take a moment to make sure we're thinking big enough. Elisha's
example would imply that our experience of God will largely be
determined by the level of our expectation.

As Elisha and Elijah shared one last conversation, many miles
and many years from that fleeting moment when Elijah gave Elisha his cloak as he passed, they also shared the rugged intimacy of
a father and son. Their story together ended as strangely as it began,
with a chariot of fire and horses of fire separating them and Elijah
ascending in a whirlwind.

Yet, as Elijah ascended, God delivered on the very thing Elisha
had asked for: a double portion of Elijah's anointing.

Elijah was regarded as the most powerful prophet in the history of God's people. His miracles were unparalleled, his stories unprecedented. So for a guy like Elisha, who had spent the prime years of his life plowing with oxen, having *any* portion in what God did in Elijah would surely have been sufficient. But Elisha didn't ask for Elijah's portion. It wasn't Elijah's portion value-sized for an additional seventy-nine cents. It was *double* the anointing.

And most astounding of all, God agreed. God didn't want Elisha to simply share in Elijah's miracles—God wanted to give him something greater. Greater signs, greater wonders, greater authority, greater faith.

I don't know whether Elisha had second thoughts before he committed holy arson by putting his plow and oxen in the flames and then following Elijah. But the outcome of his obedience would be evident to everyone years later when he was performing double the number of Elijah's miracles.

🔁 RT Don't look down on your God-given potential as if the really powerful stuff is meant just for others, not you. #GreaterBook

---

Anytime you start having second thoughts and are tempted to tap out and get back to the predictable beat of the ordinary, it can be helpful to consider what's at stake:

- Greater authority and confidence in God than you've ever known
- Greater clarity of your identity and your calling

- Greater purpose as you approach everyday tasks
- Greater joy in knowing that you're in the sweet spot of God's blessing
- Greater influence with the people around you
- Greater impact in the world

Don't look down on your God-given potential, as if the really powerful stuff is meant just for others, not you. Now, the greater calling that God has for you may not be outwardly impressive or publicly visible. But that doesn't mean it won't be high impact in its own way.

Expand your vision. *You* can do something great. Times two.

PRAYER FOCUS: Be bold and ask God for something really important to do for Him today.

Strike the Water

*[Elisha] took the cloak that had fallen from Elijah and
struck the water with it. "Where now is the Lord, the
God of Elijah?" he asked. When he struck the water, it
divided to the right and to the left, and he crossed over.*

—2 Kings 2:14

Today's Bible reading: 2 Kings 2:13–18

Today's verses pick up right where we left off yesterday. Elisha
had received a double portion of Elijah's spirit, and he was about
to prove it.

He picked up the cloak that had fallen from Elijah and walked
back to the edge of the river. He lifted the cloak high above his
head and with all his might brought it down in an arc...

Strike!

After that moment history was rewritten—Elisha's history and
that of everyone who came into contact with him. God would
show Himself just as strongly for Elisha as He had for Elijah. This
prophet, in fact, went on to do twice as many miracles as his
mentor.

Yet I believe the primary significance of Elisha's striking the

Jordan River had little to do with the *activity* he would go on to do and everything to do with the *identity* God wanted to establish in him.

Here's why. Identity always comes before activity in the order of God. Before Elisha could go on to do greater things, he had to have a "baptism" (if we can call it that) in the affirmation of God, just as the Father affirmed Jesus at His baptism (see Mark 1:9–11). The parting of the water showed that the same God who had worked miracles through Elijah was now working through Elisha. He was a prophet accepted by God.

When you know who God is, and He shows you who you are, you will know what to do. Identity, then activity.

Perhaps, when you think about yourself, you tend to have in mind the times you've sinned and disappointed God and others. Or the way you lack the gifts and advantages others seem to have. *That person can't have a great role in God's works in the world,* you think.

RT When you know who God is, and He shows you who you are, you will know what to do. #GreaterBook

---

But you're *not* that person.

You're not defined by your failures and limitations but instead by the presence of God within you. Your identity is child of God. Your nature is righteousness through Christ. Your destination is eternity in God's love.

The past is past. However old you are, whatever has gone on in former years for you, the future holds something different. And you, yourself, are changing to meet it.

Repeatedly in the Scriptures, the Jordan River represents transition. Think of the children of Israel, under General Joshua, crossing to conquer the Promised Land. Or Jesus being baptized by John. So when Elisha crossed over to the other side of the Jordan, he was transitioning from apprentice to prophet with a double anointing.

You, too, are in the process of transition. Your walk with Jesus is all about progress. You are going from glory to glory by the transforming power of the Spirit (see 2 Corinthians 3:18).

As you are standing at the Jordan River today, don't test the water. Don't tap the water. Don't put your toe in the water.

Strike the water.

Then go forward, advancing in the journey that God has called you to.

PRAYER FOCUS: Ask God to affirm your identity in Christ within your heart and to help you live in a way that's consistent with who you are and who you are becoming.

Don't Drown in a Kiddie Pool

Jesus immediately said to them: "Take courage! It is I.
Don't be afraid."

"Lord, if it's you," Peter replied, "tell me to come
to you on the water."

"Come," he said.

—MATTHEW 14:27–29

Today's Bible reading: Matthew 14:22–33

"What if I fail?"

That's one of the most frequent questions that surfaces when it comes to living a life of risk and following God's vision.

What if it doesn't work? What if I take this big step of faith and it doesn't get me anywhere? What if I set a huge goal and I fall short? What if I take the plunge and drown?

I'm not going to lie to you, it's possible. Otherwise, it wouldn't be a risk. There is no offer of certainty. No guarantee that it's going to work. That your step is going to land. That your goal is going to be met. That you aren't going to drown in your attempt to launch out in faith.

But here's a perspective that's helped me.

Personally, if I'm going to drown, I want to drown in deep water. When taking a risk, if I'm going to go down—and I may—at least I want to be in the deep end when I do it.

In other words, I don't want to drown in a kiddie pool.

There's a greater risk than taking a risk and failing. And that's taking none and failing. And maybe even worse, taking none and succeeding.

Peter had the idea. Or maybe he wasn't really thinking at all; I don't know. But his instinct was right—*If Jesus is out there on the water, I want to be out there too.* He took the all-important first step over the side of the boat. It didn't matter how deep the water was.

The greatest risk you can take in your life is to risk nothing with your life. To live life in the kiddie pool. To make your ultimate ambition a completely safe life. Because then if you fail, it's embarrassing. And if you succeed, it's insulting to a God who had much bigger things in mind for your life.

RT The greatest risk you can take in your life is to risk nothing with your life. #GreaterBook

---

Failure is a possibility no matter what you do. So is success. Whatever happens, I want my life to be marked by a willingness to wade deeper and find out.

PRAYER FOCUS: Ask for greater faith and courage to dive into the deep waters of high-risk, high-reward obedience to Christ.

Ambition and Arrogance

I press on toward the goal to win the prize for which
God has called me heavenward in Christ Jesus.

—Philippians 3:14

Today's Bible reading: Philippians 3

There's a quality that many Christians are afraid of. To utter it is almost to speak a bad word. If you have it, many people assume that means you're self-serving, power hungry, but most of all arrogant.

I'm talking about ambition.

It's almost like, if you want to excel at something or do big things with your life or organization, then you must have a God complex. An elevated sense of self-importance.

There's definitely no denying it's true in the case of some people. And I'm sure it's been true of me far too often, even in ways I'm not aware of. But I also worry that a pervasive and exaggerated fear of ambition can become an excuse for complacency.

I've seen too many pastors settle for reaching hundreds when God called them to reach thousands. I've seen too many talented businesspeople stop short of the impact God called them to make in their industries. All because they feared being thought of as ambitious.

So let's clear this up once and for all: *nowhere* in the Bible is ambition condemned. *Selfish* ambition is certainly warned against. But ambition for the sake of God's glory is not only condoned, but it's commended. It's a required asset for anyone wanting to step out and do something extraordinary.

It required some ambition for Noah to build the ark. For David to expand the borders of Israel. For Solomon to build the temple. For Nehemiah to rebuild the walls. For Peter to head up the early church.

Saul of Tarsus was an ambitious young man, an up-and-comer in the Jewish power structure, before the resurrected Jesus knocked him off his high horse on the road to Damascus. The thing is, he was *still* ambitious after the scales fell off his eyes. Except now he was ambitious for the gospel of Christ. Are you surprised that he spread the good news about Jesus wider than anybody else in his lifetime? He was pressing on toward his goal.

RT A pervasive and exaggerated fear of ambition can become an excuse for complacency. #GreaterBook

---

Do you think people accused Paul of being arrogant? Of course they did. But then again, if you're never accused of being arrogant, it might be a sign that you're not being ambitious enough. You're dreaming too small. Your goals are too easily attainable.

Be set free: it's not a sin to want to be the best at what you do.

It's okay for you to want to achieve as much as you can with your life for the sake of the God who gave it to you. I sincerely doubt God is going to look at you at the end of your life and say, "You did too much for Me." But I do sincerely believe that God is going to look at many people and say, "You were too falsely humble for your own good and for the good of countless people you could have impacted if you'd had a little more ambition."

Don't let anyone ever tell you that ambition is necessarily synonymous with arrogance. Godly ambition is what God uses to do greater things in our world.

PRAYER FOCUS: Ask God to purify your motives and give you the ambition to pursue great things for His sake.

Staying Out of Trouble or Walking in Your Calling?

You Pharisees clean the outside of the cup and dish, but inside you are full of greed and wickedness. You foolish people! Did not the one who made the outside make the inside also? But now as for what is inside you—be generous to the poor, and everything will be clean for you.

—LUKE 11:39–41

Today's Bible reading: Luke 11:37–52

Why are so many of us Christians doing so little for Christ?

Some think it's our lack of commitment. Others think it's because we're not equipped well enough.

I don't think it's that or anything like that.

What's the problem?

We aren't moving toward something worthy of giving ourselves completely over to. Instead, we've settled for simply trying to keep ourselves out of trouble. We try to obey this rule, keep ourselves separate from that, and boycott the other thing. It's like we're children and we're still trying to be good little boys and girls.

God did not raise us up for that. He wants to make us great men and women of God. Of course, morality and purity matter, but they're not the primary reason we're here on the earth. God has placed a calling on our lives, collectively and individually. And this is what we need to spend all of our time and energy pursuing. We do not need to be behavioral modification specialists. We need to walk in our calling.

RT We don't, first and foremost, need rules to live by. We need a calling to live for. #GreaterBook

---

Perhaps our faith is ineffective because we're responding to an anemic version of the gospel. The vision we are embracing is too weak. The challenge we are accepting isn't great enough. We are lulled to sleep with dos and don'ts instead of waking up to the God-given potential inside us. This was Jesus's gripe with the religious leaders of His day who insisted on obedience to a multitude of rules but didn't actually do anything good for the kingdom's sake.

The truth is, you can stay out of trouble but fall short of your calling. You can stay out of trouble while living a life of little impact or significance.

When we come to understand that God has something for us far greater than rule keeping, everything changes. And it goes far beyond staying out of trouble. Our motivation is that we would not dare risk the glorious destiny God has for us by wasting our time on anything that could short-circuit it, whether that's sin or excessive sin consciousness.

We don't, first and foremost, need rules to live by. We need a calling to live for. And that calling is empowered by the grace of God.

PRAYER FOCUS: If you have been either lax or legalistic in your attitude toward sin, ask God to show you the *true* source of the issue.

Avoiding a 13:13 Moment

"You have done a foolish thing," Samuel said. "You have not kept the command the LORD your God gave you; if you had, he would have established your kingdom over Israel for all time."

—1 SAMUEL 13:13

Today's Bible reading: 1 Samuel 13:1–14

King Saul felt he needed a word of encouragement from the Lord, but when he got tired of waiting for the prophet Samuel to show up for the religious ceremony, he went ahead and did it himself.

Shortly afterward, Samuel arrived and gave him the rebuke we find in 1 Samuel 13:13.

What a scary verse that is. Besides the fact that here we have a double instance of a traditionally unlucky number, the thought expressed in the verse should rattle us to our core.

Let me explain what I mean.

When most people talk about the consequences of sin or disobeying a specific instruction of God, they focus on the negative consequences that could happen as a result. You sleep around, and you could get an STD or get pregnant. You cut a corner at work, and you could lose your job. You miss church too many times in a row, and you'll be forced to listen to the Canadian rock band Nickelback for eight straight hours. Scary stuff.

Kidding aside, while those are definitely bad consequences, there's an even scarier thought to consider, namely, the unprecedented blessing of God you missed out on because you weren't willing to obey. The levels of influence you could have had. The marriage you could have enjoyed. The grace you could have experienced. The life you could have led.

Although Israel's first king, Saul, wasn't willing to completely carry out God's instructions, eventually there would come another king—David—who would not settle for less. Who would procure a greater destiny through an unstinting, passionate pursuit of the plan of God. David, not Saul, was a man after God's own heart. David, not Saul, would have the house that would not end, because King Jesus would be his descendant.

RT The last thing you want your life to become is a cautionary tale of what could have been. #GreaterBook

---

A 13:13 moment—it's a moment you never want to have. A moment when you realize you let a chance for something greater slip out of your grasp. A moment when you realize just what you could have had if only you had...

I never want to have a 13:13 moment. I never want to hear

God say, "If you had been generous, I would have..." "If you had not settled, I would have..." "If you had stepped out in faith, I would have..."

And I know you don't want to hear those things either. The last thing you want your life to become is a life like Saul's—a cautionary tale of what could have been.

It's the last thing God wants for you too. Whatever He is asking of you as He calls you to greater things, it's not about what He wants *from* you. It's about what He wants *for* you.

And you can have it, if only you will...

PRAYER FOCUS: Figure out what the "If only I will..." is for you, then ask God's help to take your next step of obedience.

Shovel-Ready Miracle

*[Elisha] said, "Thus says the LORD: 'Make this valley
full of ditches.' For thus says the LORD: 'You shall not
see wind, nor shall you see rain; yet that valley shall
be filled with water, so that you, your cattle, and your
animals may drink.'"*

—2 KINGS 3:16–17, NKJV

Today's Bible reading: 2 Kings 3:9–24

The kings of Israel, Judah, and Edom had put together a military
force that should have been fearsome against the Moabites—until
they almost immediately ran out of water for their armies and animals. That's when they went looking for Elisha.

He confirmed to the kings that water would be flowing from
Edom by the time the sun came up the next morning. But he told
them to take a small, pretty ludicrous step first: dig ditches.

Why would anybody in their right mind dig ditches to hold
rain that isn't even in the forecast?

Well, the actual Hebrew language that is translated "make this
valley full of ditches" was likely idiomatic. It probably wasn't a lit-

eral command for the Israelites to dig. But it is a helpful picture of how faith works.

When you know God has promised you greater things, you don't wait for a sign to appear before you respond. The kings wanted a miracle. They would get their miracle. But first they got a work order: This is no time for the power of positive thinking. This is the time to tie a bandanna around your head and pick up a shovel.

I think this image of ditch digging can be used to teach us an important paradox of great faith: Only God can send the rain. But He expects you to dig the ditches.

It gets the message across that if you want God to do the super, you're going to have to do the natural. If you don't move, God won't move.

RT When you know God has promised you greater things, you don't wait for a sign to appear before you respond. #GreaterBook

---

Everybody wants to achieve greater things. They want God to give them great success. But it's kind of like the difference between somebody who plays Guitar Hero and a real guitar player. Everybody wants to be a rock star, but not everybody wants to learn the chords. Everybody wants a miracle, but few want to do the work to prepare for the miracle.

If you're looking for something greater in a relationship, do you need to dig a ditch by speaking a word over that relationship? Just as Genesis tells us that God created our world from a spoken word, He also can create new worlds in your life through the words you speak.

Do you want something greater in your finances? Then dig a ditch by starting to pay off your debt.

Do you want victory over sin in your life? Dig a ditch by memorizing Scripture.

Now, here's something encouraging for you. There is no correlation between the Israelites' ability to dig an irrigation system and God's ability to send rain. Yet the very next morning, water came flooding into those ditches (see verse 20).

When you don't feel like you have enough faith to do what God has called you to do, the simple act of taking a step can be enough to cause God to act in your life. Right now, you don't need to have enough faith to finish. You just need to have enough faith to get started.

PRAYER FOCUS: Is there a ditch you can dig today in preparation for the rain that you're expecting tomorrow? Ask God for the faith to do that much.

Shut Up and Get Moving

Moses answered the people,…"The LORD will fight for you; you need only to be still."

Then the LORD said to Moses, "Why are you crying out to me? Tell the Israelites to move on."

—EXODUS 14:13–15

Today's Bible reading: Exodus 14

Exodus 14:14 is one of the most misinterpreted verses in the Bible. Most of us, including me, have looked at it as a faith-infusing verse of what we should do when we need help or a breakthrough. When we're looking for God to do something big. When we're waiting to see God bring something new and greater into our lives.

Be still. Let the Lord fight the battle for you. Let go and let God. In short, do nothing.

There's just one problem with that: verse 15.

In verse 14, Moses tells the people that God will fight for them and that they are to be still. But in verse 15, God comes in and immediately contradicts Moses. He doesn't tell the people to stand still. He tells them to shut up and get moving. Into the sea.

Moses was wrong. In isolation, verse 14 is wrong. Yes, God's going to fight for them. But it won't be while they're standing there and doing nothing. It's in the parted sea. It's while they're moving that God will be fighting.

RT It can be easy to think we should stand still and cry out when God is actually looking for us to shut up and get moving. #GreaterBook

---

Sometimes it can be easy to mistake passivity for patience, laziness for faith.

Sometimes it can be easy to think we should stand still and cry out when God is actually looking for us to shut up and get moving. Not to do everything on our own, obviously. But to realize that faith isn't necessarily sitting and waiting for God to do everything on His own for us. God fights while we move.

For example, if you're unemployed, it isn't faith for you to stay at home and watch the Food Network while praying during commercial breaks and expecting God to throw a job into your lap. Faith is updating your résumé. Getting yourself out the door. And applying for jobs. Letting God fight for you in your job search.

You could apply this to pretty much every area of your life. Relationships. Finances. Major life decisions.

Faith isn't passive. It's active. If you don't believe me, read Hebrews 11. I defy you to find one verse that says, "By faith, they watched." It's always by faith, they moved. By faith, they did.

That's because faith is knowing who God is, *acting* accordingly, and then *watching* Him act accordingly.

PRAYER FOCUS: Activate your prayer today by praying while you're in the midst of doing something to fulfill God's present call in your life.

Daydreams and Sweatshops

*God saw all that he had made, and it was
very good.*

—Genesis 1:31

Today's Bible reading: Genesis 1:1–2:3

I was recently reading Robert McKee's book on the process of
storytelling and came across a sentence that challenged me. He
was discussing the hard work of the creative endeavor and constructing fictional environments, and he said, "Worlds are not daydreams but sweatshops."

It got me thinking in a similar vein about how we often mis-
understand the concept of having a vision from God. For our lives,
for our ministries, and really for everything in general.

I believe that when most people think or talk about getting a
vision from God, it's more along the lines of a daydream. We as-
sociate receiving a vision from God with being passive. We think
that God speaks to us with candles lit and music playing.

He often does. But that's not where the vision comes to life. It's simply the moment of conception.

The vision really comes to life when the candles go out and the music stops. It's when we have to get down to the hard work of actually making it happen. Visions don't come to life in daydreams but in sweatshops.

If you're a church planter, it's in the hours you spend setting up your portable location just to be able to preach for forty minutes. If God has called you to be a doctor, it's in the years of schooling and interning that you have to endure to get those two simple letters, MD, attached to your name. If you're a writer or a filmmaker, it's in the days and months of brainstorming, executing, and editing it takes to make your project a reality.

RT Visions don't come to life in daydreams but in sweatshops. #GreaterBook

---

Being a visionary or receiving a vision isn't defined simply by what you can think of. A child can think of a lot of things that have no chance of becoming real. Being a visionary has to do with what you can bring to life.

God is the Creator, not because He imagined or envisioned creation, but because He acted and brought it into existence. He expressed intense satisfaction in doing the work and seeing the final product. Why should it be any different for the creatures who were made in His image?

So, is your vision more like an airy daydream or a blueprint for construction? Are you indulging in fantasies from a recliner or working up a sweat to make your vision a reality?

Go build a world.

PRAYER FOCUS: If you've been daydreaming about what you would like to do differently, without putting any muscle behind it, confess and repent. (To repent means to change your behavior.)

And Then Some

Let your light shine before others, that they may see
your good deeds and glorify your Father in heaven.

—Matthew 5:16

Today's Bible reading: Matthew 5:13–16

What is the secret to doing anything worthwhile or significant in life? It's not natural aptitude. As nice it may be to have been born with skills and talents, they will only take you so far on their own. No, at the end of the day, it's your drive to go above and beyond that is going to set you apart from the masses who live in the muck of mediocrity.

I've found there are three types of people when it comes to motivation. Each person puts forth a certain kind of effort, and each person receives a corresponding reward.

- People in the first category have a *bare minimum mentality.* These are D- persons, doing enough to pass but nothing more. They spend the bare minimum time with their spouse that it takes to appease him or her. They turn in work that meets the bare minimum requirements. And then they wonder why their marriage fails, they never get a promotion, and they can never find fulfillment in life.

- The second group of people run by the mantra of *good enough*. These are B people, and they are numerous. They turn in work that shows effort. They do the routine daily and weekly duties that set them up for a good marriage or a good job performance. But they leave it at that.

- And then there are people with *world-class drive*. They're A+ people. Good enough isn't good enough for them when they know they have God's Spirit within them. They are committed to excellence. They want to exceed expectations. As a result, they generally have great jobs, great marriages, and greater fulfillment.

What sets this last group of people apart really comes down to three simple words: *and then some*.

RT At the end of the day, it's your drive to go above and beyond that is going to set you apart from the masses. #GreaterBook

---

People with world-class drive who reap world-class rewards do what they're supposed to do *and then some*. They don't get flowers for their spouse just on their anniversary; they also do it on random days for no reason at all. They don't just do what they're asked to do at work; they find ways to go above and beyond. They don't just volunteer once a month for a team at church; they find an overlooked need, throw their energy into it, and make a real difference in Jesus's name.

These people are not tasteless salt or hidden lights (see Matthew 5:13–16). Their hearts don't have a nauseous lukewarm temperature, neither hot nor cold, that makes Christ want to spit them out of His mouth (see Revelation 3:15–16). These are "work heartily, as for the Lord" people (Colossians 3:23–24, ESV).

Choose to live your life with an "and then some" mentality. Reject mediocrity. Don't let good enough be good enough for you when you have God in you. Your calling is greater than that.

PRAYER FOCUS: If you've been settling for good enough—or worse, bare minimum—pray for God's power to boost you to the higher level of "and then some" in all you do.

Your Exceptional Exception

Elisha replied to her, "How can I help you? Tell me, what do you have in your house?"

"Your servant has nothing there at all," she said, "except a small jar of olive oil."

—2 Kings 4:2

Today's Bible reading: 2 Kings 4:1–7

All this woman could focus on was what she didn't have. Elisha, on the other hand, was interested in her exception. And it was her exception that became the vessel for a miracle.

People often excuse themselves from the miraculous because they don't have a lot to work with or to offer God to work with. Maybe it's their lack of skills. An absence of resources. Little experience.

Whatever the reason, what they don't realize is that their lack in itself makes them candidates for the power of God to flow through their lives.

God has a history of using what little someone has to do great things only He can do. God used a shepherd's staff to part the Red Sea (see Exodus 14:15–22). He used five loaves and two fish to feed thousands (see Mark 6:30–44). He even used a donkey to talk to someone and save his life (see Numbers 22:21–35).

RT All God needs to work miracles in your life is all you have. #GreaterBook

---

One of the greatest strategies of the Enemy is to get you to focus on what you don't have, what you used to have, or what someone else has that you wish you had. Instead of going down that dead-end path, you should look in your house and ask the question, "God, what can You do through what I have?"

So you don't have the opportunity to stand onstage at a football stadium and preach the gospel like Billy Graham. Who works in your office and needs to know the love of Christ? Share it with them.

So you don't have the money to write a huge check to a ministry you believe in. A small monthly pledge might be just the thing to stretch your faith while making a big difference through meeting a small need.

So you don't have the experience necessary to get a new job in a more exciting field. You may be picking up some wax-on-wax-off skills and disciplines that will pave the way for your future in a way you aren't meant to understand now.

Here's the profound truth we must begin embracing today: all God needs to work miracles in our lives is all we have. A God who created something out of nothing when He birthed the universe can also create something great out of something little in your life.

Like the widow of Shunem who had only a little oil for Elisha and like the widow Jesus praised for contributing her last pennies to the temple (see Mark 12:41–44), give all you've got, however small it is.

God can do exceptional things with your exception.

PRAYER FOCUS: Spend some time thinking about what you *do* have to offer God, not what you *don't*. Then, in prayer, offer it all to Him.

Upon Further Review

When Elisha reached the house, there was the boy
lying dead on his couch.... As he stretched himself
out on him, the boy's body grew warm. Elisha turned
away and walked back and forth in the room and then
got on the bed and stretched out on him once more.
The boy sneezed seven times and opened his eyes.

—2 KINGS 4:32, 34–35

Today's Bible reading: 2 Kings 4:8–37

Have you ever watched a football game when a coach challenges a
ruling on the field? It usually happens because a call is close and
they need to review the play to make sure the referee got it right.
Sometimes the official confirms the ruling on the field. But at
other times, because of something the official upstairs sees that the
referees couldn't see on the field, he overturns the ruling. It turns
out to be a touchdown after all. The receiver was in bounds. And
the official reverses the original verdict.

In other words, upon further review, everything changes.

The referee's call that the Shunammite woman's son was dead
turned out to be reversible upon further review. The exact same

thing was true when Jesus was put in a tomb—His resurrection was the greatest reversal in human history.

So, in your life, you need to remember that the first report isn't always the final report, especially when you're living out God's greater vision for your life. There will always be a lesser opinion from somebody else, even from yourself. It can come from your past. It can come from some of the issues and hang-ups that keep you feeling down. But there's always a greater perspective that God sees from His replay booth in heaven, and His perspective always prevails in the end.

RT In situations that feel wasted, wrapped in sorrow, cold to the touch, God has the power to bring forth one thousand new lives. #GreaterBook

---

Every dead area of your life is under further review when you send it upstairs to the God who has a higher vantage point and sees your situation from angles you can't access. So what is the situation in your life that seems dead and has you feeling defeated?

Maybe a relationship in your life just fell apart.

Maybe you lost your job last year.

Maybe you've made some terrible mistakes that have cost you a lot of time and opportunity.

Whatever the situation is, it's not over as long as Jesus is on the scene.

Upon further review, He can restore the relationship.

Upon further review, He can supply all your needs.

Upon further review, He can forgive you and make you whole.

Most of us give up too soon on the greater life God has for us. Don't lose hope. With God, nothing in your life is ever beyond resuscitation. And even in situations that feel wasted, wrapped in sorrow, cold to the touch, He has the power to bring forth one thousand new lives.

PRAYER FOCUS: Call a coach's challenge in your life. Ask God to reverse the apparent disappointing results in your life, resurrecting your hope.

Think Inside the Box

"We have here only five loaves of bread and two fish,"
[the disciples] answered.
  "Bring them here to me," [Jesus] said.

—Matthew 14:17–18

Today's Bible reading: Matthew 14:13–21

When it comes to our limitations, most people operate out of an if-then mind-set. *If* I had more money, *then* I would buy a nicer house. *If* I could sing, *then* I would be a musician. *If* my children were in a different stage of life, *then* I would move. *If* my church had a state-of-the-art facility, *then* we would grow.

You encounter this same kind of thinking in the corporate world. It's called "thinking outside the box." It's used deliberately in brainstorming, and it's a way of imagining how to break out of restraints and do more.

Sounds nice, but this mind-set is a breeding ground for frustration. Why? Because for the time being, the *then* is impossible since you don't have the *if.* You don't have unlimited money. You can't sing. Your children aren't in a different stage of life. And your church still has the same building.

In other words, for now, you're stuck with your limitations. And while it might be liberating to think about life as if you didn't have these limitations, they're still there and you have to work with them.

I'm not saying you shouldn't plan ahead or you shouldn't dream. Of course you should. But your box is never going to expand to the place where you're thinking outside of it until you learn to live within it.

I would challenge you to think inside the box. Stop waiting for what you want and work with what you've got. How much money do you have? What talents has God given you? How can you maximize your church or corporation with the assets and resources you currently have?

RT Your greatest limitation is God's greatest opportunity. #GreaterBook

---

The disciples only saw the lunchbox of food they had to feed a crowd with. Jesus saw what His Father could do with this start.

In a very similar miracle, Elisha multiplied a small supply of grain for a hundred men, with leftovers to spare (see 2 Kings 4:42–44). His limitations weren't so limiting after all.

Your greatest limitation is God's greatest opportunity. If He wanted you to have _____, He would have provided it to you. If He wanted you to do _____, He would have made you able. But if He didn't, there must be something greater in mind that He wants to do through your limitation. He must have something in mind He wants to do with what you actually have and actually can do.

Most of us are so focused on what we don't have that we're blinded to what we do have. If you had all the resources you think you needed, maybe you wouldn't be forced to draw upon the unseen resources God has actually put inside of you.

And what He has put inside of you is all you need to accomplish all that He's called you to do.

Even if it seems limited to you.

PRAYER FOCUS: Pray for God to multiply the effectiveness of whatever you have to offer Him this day.

The Compound Effect

If you possess these qualities in increasing measure,
they will keep you from being ineffective and unpro-
ductive in your knowledge of our Lord Jesus Christ.

—2 PETER 1:8

Today's Bible reading: 2 Peter 1:3–11

While reading, I recently encountered an idea called *the principle of compound effect*. The basic concept is that small but consistent habits and incremental changes add up to pay big rewards over time.

For example, putting a dollar a day into a mutual fund might not seem like a big investment. But over time, the accumulated deposits and their dividends will add up to a sum exponentially greater than the initial investment.

From my experience, this principle isn't limited to the realm of finances or business practices. It applies to every area of life. Your work ethic. Your relationships. Your personal development. Even your walk with God.

Most people tend to take the approach of trying to make large periodic investments in order to initiate growth in these areas. And usually because they have fallen behind. You get behind on your work, so you wake up every morning at four for a week to get caught up. Your marriage is struggling, so you go to a conference. You feel distant from God, so you rededicate your life.

RT It's often the smallest things done consistently that have the potential to change everything for the greater. #GreaterBook

---

Sometimes it's necessary to do these things. But rather than having to periodically overhaul your life to make up for deficiencies, adopting the smallest daily habits might be the better path toward excellence and long-term sustainable growth. Anyone can put in a lot of work for a short amount of time to get their game back up to par. But the people who do this usually slip afterward because they did not learn to do the small things that could have kept them moving forward the whole time.

I've recently challenged my staff to begin improving their areas of responsibility by just 1 percent every day. To be 1 percent better in their communication, their efficiency, their performance, and to challenge the people they lead to do the same.

One percent is manageable, identifiable, and attainable. And it's a daily increase and deposit that over time will take our church to an exponentially greater level than the work we're putting in to get there. Without our ever losing a step and having to make up ground.

In your own life, imagine what would happen if you committed to improving yourself by 1 percent a day every day for the next year. If you committed to improving your parenting abilities. Or the way you love and honor your spouse. Or your eating habits. Or your spiritual disciplines.

Nothing would be drastically different initially. But a year from now you would be shocked by how far you've come. And that's because it's often the smallest things done consistently that have the potential to change everything for the greater.

PRAYER FOCUS: Make a promise to God that you will steadily, bit by bit, improve in the godly living He has called you to.

Stephen the Waiter

*The Twelve gathered all the disciples together and said,
"It would not be right for us to neglect the ministry of
the word of God in order to wait on tables. Brothers
and sisters, choose seven men from among you who
are known to be full of the Spirit and wisdom. We will
turn this responsibility over to them."...*

*They chose Stephen, a man full of faith and of the
Holy Spirit.*

—Acts 6:2–3, 5

Today's Bible reading: Acts 6:1–7

From beginning to end, the book of Acts reads like a chronicle of
people used by God to accomplish the seemingly impossible.

Peter preaches at Pentecost and sees three thousand converted.
The disciples heal so many people that the sick are brought into the
streets so the disciples' shadows might fall on them. Philip tele-
ports after preaching the gospel. Paul threatens the entire socioeconomic stability of a city with his preaching, raises a dead kid to
life, gets up from a stoning, survives a shipwreck, and goes to Rome
to appear before Caesar.

But then you have Stephen. Who waits on tables for widows.

Doesn't seem very noteworthy. But never underestimate God's ability to use small, seemingly insignificant assignments to set the stage for significant impact.

If you read on in the story, Stephen begins doing great wonders among the people. There's no indication that he's vacated his post of waiting on tables. So we can probably assume he's doing miracles in the midst of his mundane duties.

Apparently he's so powerful that the local officials need to shut him up. So they bring up false charges and make him defend himself. In front of the high priest.

So what does this waiter have to say to the Jewish scholars and powerbrokers of his day? A lot. He ends up preaching the longest recorded sermon in the book of Acts.

RT Never underestimate God's ability to use small, seemingly insignificant assignments to set the stage for significant impact. #GreaterBook

---

Not Peter. Not Paul. Not any of the other apostles. But Stephen the waiter.

He preaches so powerfully that the authorities kill him. A tragic ending for Stephen, but by far his most significant moment. And that's because the ensuing persecution that comes from Stephen's sermon and death forces the church out of Judea and into Samaria and eventually into Gentile territory, where the gospel flourishes and spawns a worldwide movement.

That's exponential impact, but it all started with waiting on tables for widows.

What tables are you waiting on right now? What insignificant assignments are you having to carry out that feel like they're beneath the destiny God has in mind for you?

Don't ever forget that what starts as an insignificant assignment often leads to your most significant moment.

PRAYER FOCUS: Ask God to show you the area of service He has for you, however mundane it may be, so that you can be a serious part of the spread of His great kingdom.

Obedience and Opportunity

Whoever can be trusted with very little can also be trusted with much, and whoever is dishonest with very little will also be dishonest with much.

—Luke 16:10

Today's Bible reading: Luke 16:1–15

There's a major misconception about how God gives opportunities to His people to do something for Him. Many people want God to *first* give them great opportunities so they can display great obedience. But often, until then, they won't be obedient with what they've already been given.

Maybe it's the church planter who wants to preach to five thousand people before he'll preach with faithfulness and excellence to five hundred people. Or fifty people. Or five people.

Maybe it's the person who would love for God to give him one million dollars to be generous with, but he won't be generous with the paycheck he is receiving right now.

Maybe it's the college student who claims she would die for her faith in the Middle East, but she can't share her faith with her roommate.

If you read the Bible, it's pretty clear that this is simply not the way it works with God.

- Joseph had to be faithful in slavery and prison before he was put in charge over Egypt.
- David had to herd sheep before he killed a giant.
- And as we saw yesterday, Stephen had to wait tables for widows before he defended his faith to the masses.

Are you waiting for a great opportunity, certain that you'll be faithful when the time comes but not bothering to develop your readiness right now? You're probably not *un*faithful, but are you *less* faithful in your present responsibilities than you could be? Cutting corners? Stopping at adequate rather than going all the way to exceptional?

RT Obedience creates opportunity, not the other way around. #GreaterBook

---

God won't give you more to do for Him until you do what He's already given you to do. So stop praying for a life of impact and do something as impactful as you can. Stop praying for a bigger platform and use the one you've been given. Stop praying for a better assignment and pour more passion into the one you have.

Obedience creates opportunity, not the other way around.

Do something right now with what you have and watch the miraculous power of God multiply what you have. Be obedient with what God has given you, and He'll give you more to be obedient with.

PRAYER FOCUS: Commit before God to be faithful today, tomorrow, and from now on in whatever task He puts before you.

Pearls and Seeds

A man scatters seed on the ground. Night and day,
whether he sleeps or gets up, the seed sprouts and
grows.

—Mark 4:26–27

Today's Bible reading: Mark 4:1–20, 26–32

One of the greatest hindrances to the development of our full potential is the curse of the immediate and the obvious.

We've conditioned ourselves to believe that the best wisdom, the best way of life—the best anything, really—is something we can recognize right away. Or that is helpful to us right away. I call it the pearl-of-wisdom way of thinking.

Think of the expression "a pearl of wisdom." It refers to a saying that immediately and succinctly sounds true. That's what we want. Pearls of wisdom. Or really, just pearls, period. Things that have immediate and obvious value. A marriage that you can put on the shelf and show off. A job where everything is easy. A church with supersonic growth from day one.

The problem is that God doesn't always work that way. God *will* sometimes give you pearls—and when He does, be thankful.

But from my experience, God's wisdom or God's work in your life usually comes in the form of a seed, not a pearl.

Plant growth was one of Jesus's favorite images to portray what happens when the seed of the gospel is planted in people's lives. You could say it's the original illustration for the start-small-grow-big philosophy underlying the greater life. When God's Word takes root, its potential for creating transformation is immense.

RT Don't uproot what God is planting in you. Let Him grow it in His time. #GreaterBook

---

But first a seed has to go into the dirt to develop. It takes time. The seed doesn't have the obvious value that a pearl does. But that doesn't mean it isn't significant. A seed has latent and potential power. It doesn't look like much immediately, but over time its true worth shows itself.

So maybe you go through a rough season in your marriage. Maybe you're reassigned to a department at work where your talents aren't used to their full extent. Maybe your church is barely puttering along.

And your first thought is that maybe you've made a mistake and it's time to bail. Maybe it's no longer God's will for you to be in the marriage. At the job. In your church. Maybe you're just not cut out for this.

Maybe.

Or maybe your problem is that you're looking for a pearl. God, on the other hand, is trying to give you a seed in the form of the experiences He is giving you. The opportunities He is putting before you. The challenges He is throwing at you.

Maybe God has something better for you on the other side—a marriage that can go the distance, a better appreciation for your job, a stronger church—that you'll only get if you'll just be patient and let the seed come to life.

Don't uproot what God is trying to plant in you. Don't just wait for a pearl that you can set on a shelf. Let God put seed in the ground. And let Him grow it in His time. Believe me, you'll be thankful for the harvest when it finally comes.

PRAYER FOCUS: Pray for God to plant seeds of future spiritual greatness in you. And pray for a farmer's patience to let them sprout, grow, and mature to ripeness.

Every Step an Arrival

*Who dares despise the day of small things, since the
seven eyes of the L*ORD *that range throughout the earth
will rejoice when they see the chosen capstone in the
hand of Zerubbabel?*

—ZECHARIAH 4:10

Today's Bible reading: Zechariah 4:1–10

The Jews who had returned from exile in Babylon knew Jerusalem
was nothing like the impressive metropolis it had once been. So it
was easy for them to get depressed and think they were living in a
"day of small things." And in fact, when Zerubbabel completed the
new temple, many people rejoiced loudly. But the old-timers wept
just as loudly because they were disappointed in this new temple,
so much less glorious than the temple of Solomon that had once
stood in its place (see Ezra 3:7–13).

Zechariah's message seems to be, "Hey, at least there is a temple to worship in now!" It made more sense to see this so-called
day of small things as a day of new beginnings.

How about us? Do we consider our accomplishments to be

insignificant? What if we celebrated each achievement instead of getting down on ourselves?

↻ RT Every step you take is a victory. A chance for celebration. #GreaterBook

---

I was recently reading a book with a subtitle that grabbed me: *Every Step an Arrival,* based on a line of poetry by Denise Levertov. What the author meant by using this line is that it's great to have goals, aspirations. But the problem is that we can be so consumed with the end game that we forget that every step we take is not just a means to a distant end. It's the arrival at an end in itself. Even if a temporary one.

For example, if you're an addict, the end goal is to be free of your addiction. And it should be. But every step you take on the way to that goal is itself an arrival at a desirable destination. And that's because it's a step further away from where you don't want to be—engrossed in your addiction—and a step toward freedom. It's also a chance to experience God's grace, even in your failure.

Or if you're a pastor, you might have a goal to see your attendance double. And that's great. But you also need to understand that, when it increases by 5 percent, it's something that's worth celebrating in and of itself. Not just a number you have to go through to get to your goal.

Or in your walk with God, you're not going to become C. S. Lewis overnight. Or anyone else you look up to. And that's because neither did they. Discipleship takes time. There's never going to be a point where you're not on the road to becoming more Christlike. But even in the slow process of becoming, every step you take toward Christ is a step away from what you were without Him.

I wonder if the reason so many people give up on their goals and aspirations is that, in their lust to arrive at the end, they're blind to the fact that they're no longer at the beginning. And when they don't get to the end quickly, they conclude it's a fool's errand. Or at least a task they're not qualified to complete.

These people miss the truth we must grasp if we don't want to give up: Every step you take is a victory. A chance for celebration. A small goal that must be achieved before you can ever think about getting to a larger one.

Every step is an arrival. To think otherwise is to miss an opportunity to give God glory.

PRAYER FOCUS: Today, spend time thanking and praising God for the achievements He's brought into your life so far.

Saving Captain Awesomesauce

Naaman's servants went to him and said, "My father, if the prophet had told you to do some great thing, would you not have done it? How much more, then, when he tells you, 'Wash and be cleansed'!"

—2 Kings 5:13

Today's Bible reading: 2 Kings 5:1–14

Naaman was a rock star. Second Kings 5:1 says that he was "a great man...and highly regarded." Captain Awesomesauce has got it going on.

But in spite of Naaman's renown, he had two serious problems. His first problem was leprosy, an incurable skin disease that led to appalling disfigurement.

Naaman had heard about Elisha. And if there was even a chance this man of God could cure him, it was worth a shot. So Naaman decided to give Elisha a visit.

And here's where we begin to see Naaman's other problem—

the greater one. Pride was eating up Naaman's insides worse than the leprosy that was gnawing at his outside.

Elisha sent a messenger with the instruction for Naaman to wash seven times in the Jordan, and then he would be healed.

⮌ RT What is the one thing about which you would say, "I would do anything God asked me to do—as long as it is not that"? #GreaterBook

---

You'd think this would be the best news Naaman had heard in his entire life. A cure for his life-threatening disease! But when Naaman heard what he had to do to get healed, he flew into a rage. Dip himself in the Jordan? That muddy excuse for a river? Apparently Naaman was the Meatloaf of the Old Testament—he would do anything for healing, but he wouldn't do that.

What is the Jordan River in your life? What is the one thing about which you would say, "I would do anything God asked me to do—as long as it is not that"?

- Is it that one person you said you would never forgive?
- Is it the human achievement you need to defer to pursue something that God values more?
- Is it that potentially embarrassing conversation you need to have?
- Is it a secret sin you need to confess?
- Is it a place you would have to go, or a group of people you would have to work with, if you carried out a certain type of ministry?

One greater than Elisha wants to have a word with you immediately. His messenger—the Holy Spirit—can show you precisely the area where you need to take the dip. And every time you come up out of those waters, you'll be ready to be used by God in a greater way than ever before.

When Naaman finally lowered himself into the Jordan, it wasn't just a physical descent. He was lowering himself in obedience to God's word spoken by the lips of Elisha.

You must figure out what the dip into the river looks like for you. I can tell you this—the dip was required for Naaman to be healed. And the invitation to obedience and healing stands for each of us as well.

PRAYER FOCUS: If you're ready, tell God that you will do anything He asks you to. *Anything.* If He will empower you by His grace to do it.

The Gehazi Generation?

Was not my spirit with you when the man got down
from his chariot to meet you? Is this the time to take
money or to accept clothes—or olive groves and vine-
yards, or flocks and herds, or male and female slaves?

—2 KINGS 5:26

Today's Bible reading: 2 Kings 5:15—27

I believe we are living in one the greatest periods in history to do ministry.

We can leverage technology for the spread of the gospel in ways the apostles would never have dreamed of. The spirit of collaboration that exists between us is allowing us to share the best practices available. We're seeing things in our time that the generations that went before us longed and prayed for.

But as Luke 12:48 says, of the one to whom much is given, much is expected.

But there are distractions that can prevent us from harnessing all that we've been given to glorify God in greater ways.

Not through moral failure. Or complacency. But by chasing after the work of God for all the wrong reasons.

You can see this very real possibility in the contrasting lives of Elisha and Gehazi.

Elisha was Elijah's protégé. He was so determined to fulfill God's calling on his life that he chased after that calling with all of his heart. He wouldn't allow Elijah out of his sight. As a result, he inherited a double portion of Elijah's spirit and was used greatly by God in his generation.

RT There is no greater gift and reward for our ministry than God Himself. #GreaterBook

---

Gehazi was Elisha's protégé and should have been next in line to carry on the ministry. But instead of chasing God's calling and His glory, he chased after Naaman's gold. And because he did God's work for his own reasons, he became leprous and useless in the kingdom of God.

Sometimes I fear that my generation will become the Gehazi Generation: More interested in favors from God than the favor of God. Losing our desire to chase after God in the chase for our own glory. Pursuing God's gifts more than we pursue God Himself.

It's not that there's anything wrong with enjoying the gifts God has given us. He is a good Father, and every good and perfect gift comes from Him. However, when God's gifts become primarily about our convenience rather than our calling, we're in trouble.

But it doesn't have to be this way. We're not consigned to that fate. We can be used greatly by God if we hold onto this truth:

there is no greater gift and reward for our ministry than God Himself.

PRAYER FOCUS: Ask God to enable you to chase after His glory alone, faithfully fulfilling your calling in a world full of distractions.

Flip the Funnel

Anyone who wants to be first must be the very last,
and the servant of all.

—Mark 9:35

Today's Bible reading: Mark 9:30–37

Jesus had a lot to say about servanthood. Over and over again, He told His disciples not to be like the Gentile rulers who lorded it over the people. Instead, they were to be like servants, like children. To take seats at the bottom of the table. To wash others' feet. And Jesus had the cred to preach this message, having already left heaven and His divine prerogatives to come to earth as a lowly servant of all.

But let's make sure we understand what Jesus was really saying when He talked about servanthood.

And what He was not saying.

In my experience, a lot of people use the servanthood verses to say that we shouldn't desire to be great. To say that things like having ambition (as we mentioned in an earlier devotion), aspiring to be a leader, or wanting God to increase your platform are straight-up unbiblical and never noble.

But when you read these verses, you can't really find that idea at all. Jesus didn't say, "Stop trying to be great." He just said, "Get there a different way." Flip the funnel and put yourself at the bottom, and that's how you'll become great.

RT Jesus didn't say, "Stop trying to be great." He just said, "Get there a different way." #GreaterBook

---

You find this same idea when you study the life of John the Baptist. It's interesting that Jesus had no problem calling John the greatest man ever (see Luke 7:28). If it is bad to be great, you would think Jesus would have avoided that terminology. But once we understand why Jesus called John the Baptist the greatest man ever, it makes perfect sense. It wasn't because John was greater than Jesus. It was because he had this attitude about Jesus: "He must become greater; I must become less" (John 3:30).

There is nothing wrong with wanting to be great. In terms of your performance. Or your influence. But what you have to ask is, Why do I want to be great? How am I going to get there?

If you want to be great, be great for God's sake. If you want to be great, be great in a way that esteems Jesus as infinitely greater. If you want to be great, be a servant of all.

Flip the funnel. And start at the bottom.

PRAYER FOCUS: Ask for God to help you know better how to put Christ at the top and yourself at the bottom. Ask for the gift of humility.

Directionally Impaired

This God is our God for ever and ever;
he will be our guide even to the end.

—Psalm 48:14

Today's Bible reading: Psalm 48

I've always been directionally impaired. I could barely find my way around the house when I was growing up. When I was learning to drive, I would take the wrong turn out of my own neighborhood. Even after I got a GPS in my car, I wasn't much better at getting where I was supposed to go. The lady with the British accent often left me hanging at the most critical junctures of my journey.

Back in my college days, I was in a band that played gigs in country towns sometimes hours from where we lived. Knowing my deficiency, I would check out the directions to a venue before departing and leave with time to spare. Still, I would arrive late. Somehow I got turned around on the way. My band mates were constantly frustrated with me for this.

One of the other guys in the band—Fox—finally got fed up. "Man, you're not meeting us at the gigs anymore," he laid down the law. "I'll drive to your dorm, you and I will load up our cars with the equipment, and you will follow me all the way to the gig. That's the only way I can be sure that you're going to get there." And that's what we did.

RT The same God who brought you to this point in your life has promised to be with you to the end and be your guide. #GreaterBook

---

The thing about following Jesus in doing greater things is that, even if He tells you where to go and what to do, chances are, you won't be able to get there. You see, whether we realize it or not, we're all spiritually directionally impaired. The Bible says, "We all, like sheep, have gone astray" (Isaiah 53:6). Sheep have to be led, sometimes even carried by the shepherd.

God is our guide in a life of faithfulness and miraculous service, and we need to follow Him closely. He won't leave us behind. He'll be with us "even to the end," as Psalm 48 says.

When Fox used to lead me to those gigs, I drove a Ford Taurus, and he drove a red Pontiac Grand Am. His car was much faster than mine, but I would put my foot on the pedal and floor it to stay behind Fox, because I didn't know where I was going. My only hope was to stay behind him.

The same God who was with Elijah and Elisha, and the same God who brought you to this point in your life, has promised to be with you to the end and be your guide.

Not just to give you directions, but to direct you.

Not just to show you His will, but to show you Himself.

Not just to tell you where to go, but to empower you to get there.

You can have confidence even in the midst of uncertainty if you stay close to the Guide.

PRAYER FOCUS: Ask God to lead you, turn by turn, as you head toward the destination to which He has called you.

An Ounce of Anointing

The anointing you received from [the Son] remains in you, and you do not need anyone to teach you. But as his anointing teaches you about all things and as that anointing is real, not counterfeit—just as it has taught you, remain in him.

—1 John 2:27

Today's Bible reading: 1 John 2:18–27

An ounce of anointing is more precious than a ton of talent.

When I say "anointing," I'm talking about the supernatural enabling of the Holy Spirit. If you've got it, you will do greater things for God than you can imagine and will live a remarkable life for His glory. Without it, we can do nothing of lasting value.

In Christian speech, sometimes it seems like anointing is reserved for preachers, as in "What an anointed sermon today, Pastor!" Actually, God's anointing is for anyone who knows Christ. "You have an anointing from the Holy One," John says plainly to believers (1 John 2:20). The Holy Spirit has been freely given to us all.

If you're anointed by God and are acting in a way that's consistent with this anointing, you'll do things far beyond your capability. You'll live in a constant state of humility because you need the Lord for every step, every breath, every situation. You'll live in constant amazement at all the ways He comes through for you.

Without the anointing, even our strengths will become weaknesses in time. We'll still do what appears to be good stuff, maybe even impressive stuff. But it won't be greater stuff. It won't have eternal power in it, and it will be just a small slice of what we could have done if we really allowed the Lord to do it through us.

RT An ounce of anointing is more precious than a ton of talent. #GreaterBook

---

Talent is important. It's a gift from God. But having talent without anointing is kind of like having seat warmers in a car but not having an engine under the hood.

God can work in spite of our lack of talent. Through the anointing, even our weakness can become a playing field for the Lord to show off His strength. Ask Moses and Paul.

But talent alone isn't enough to get the job done if you don't have God's power behind it. You'll come up short in the end. Ask Samson and Saul.

I'm asking God today for a fresh anointing on my life. How about you?

PRAYER FOCUS: Ask the Father to fill you today with the Spirit so that you can experience supernatural results in His power instead of natural results in your own power.

Jesus: WYSIWYG

[Jesus] could not do any miracles there, except lay his hands on a few sick people and heal them. And he was amazed at their lack of faith.

—MARK 6:5–6

Today's Bible reading: Mark 6:1–6

Have you ever wondered why some people experience the power of God on a greater level than others? Why some people seem to be magnetic for miracles and the extraordinary, while others only hear about them? Why some people are living the greater life, while others are living a "good enough" life at best?

There are a lot of reasons, but I believe the story in Mark 6 gives us one huge aspect of the answer.

At this point in His ministry, Jesus was on a roll. In fact, in this chapter of Mark we pick up in the middle of a regional speaking tour, and Jesus was practically packing out coliseums with people who came to hear Him and be healed by Him. You would expect Him to be able to roll into His hometown and do even greater things. But that's not what happened. Instead, all He could do was heal a common cold.

Why does the Bible say Jesus couldn't do miracles? Not wouldn't, but *couldn't*?

When you read today's Bible passage, it's pretty clear. The miracle-working power of Jesus wasn't limited because His ability had subsided but because the people did not believe. And their unbelief was tied directly to what they saw. And they didn't see much.

Like many of us today, their *exposure* to Jesus was great. But also like many of us today, their *experience* of Him was limited. That's why He was amazed at their lack of faith. And that's why His power was, in a way of speaking, limited.

RT Jesus's miracle-working power hasn't changed. What may be different is whether we see that power as being available to us. #GreaterBook

---

I believe the reason some people see God show up in extraordinary measures and do remarkable things, while others are dying on the vine, has nothing to do with the power of God. God is powerful everywhere. He's powerful on every continent and in every time zone. He has the ability to change lives anywhere you go.

The determining factor in the activity of God in our lives isn't even who Jesus is. Jesus is the same yesterday, today, and forever.

It really comes down to this: *It's not who He is. It's how we see Him.*

The people of Nazareth saw Him as a carpenter. That's what

they got. Others had seen Him as someone capable of miracles. That's what they got.

The same principle is true today.

If you see Him as someone who used to move in power, that's what you're going to get. If you see Him as someone who still moves in power, that's what you're going to get.

When it comes to Jesus, in many ways it's WYSIWYG: what you see is what you get.

Jesus's infinite miracle-working power hasn't changed. It's still the same. What may be different is whether you see that power as being available to you. If you do, what can then be different is how much you will witness that power flowing through your life.

PRAYER FOCUS: Ask God to help you experience Jesus's power in the present, not just read about it in the Bible.

Don't Become Too Likely

*God chose the foolish things of the world to shame the
wise; God chose the weak things of the world to shame
the strong.*

—1 CORINTHIANS 1:27

Today's Bible reading: 1 Corinthians 1:18–31

If you look throughout the Bible, you'll notice a striking trend: God
has an affinity for the overlooked and unlikely. He likes to take
people whom no one else has noticed and raise them up to do great
things. He likes to take people who have felt underwhelmed by
their own personality and appearance and overwhelm the world
with how great He can make them by His glory and for His glory.

Noah, Abraham, Moses, David, Elisha, the disciples, Paul—all
of them were, in some ways, highly unlikely to be used by God. But
each of them was used by God, not just in spite of their weakness,
but in many cases because of their weakness.

Much of the early church was made up of people who were
less educated and low on the socioeconomic scale, even slaves. Yet
the spread of the gospel in their day puts some of our kingdom-
building efforts to shame.

Inspiring, yes?

But then consider the opposite example. Think of Uzziah. An incredibly able and successful king in Israel who enjoyed the favor of God for a season. He won countless battles. Built numerous buildings. But then, according to one of the most haunting verses in the Bible, everything turned:

> His fame spread far and wide, for he was greatly helped until he became powerful.
>
> But after Uzziah became powerful, his pride led to his downfall. (2 Chronicles 26:15–16)

It seems like the more confidence we put in the human resources we accumulate, the less likely we are to see the miracle power and potential of God in our lives. And that's because the likelier you try to become, the more unlikely it will be that God will get the glory due Him.

RT God likes to take people whom no one else has noticed and raise them up to do great things. #GreaterBook

---

Now that's bad news only if you're overflowing with talents, gifts, and opportunities. But if you feel under-resourced to do what God has called you to do, it's good news.

If you feel like you don't have the education you should have, that's good. If you feel like the town you're from would make Nazareth look like Manhattan, that's good. You are at the top of God's list as a candidate for kingdom usefulness.

When all the smoke clears and the dust settles in your life, if you're overlooked and unlikely and yet you've been a part of something far greater than the ordinary, then everybody has to credit Jesus. Everybody has to look to Him, because it could only have been Him behind it all. That's a good place to be.

Try not to become too likely. Jesus likes using the unlikely.

PRAYER FOCUS: Thank the Lord for using someone like you.

Staying Sharp

The man of God asked, "Where did it fall?" When he showed him the place, Elisha cut a stick and threw it there, and made the iron float. "Lift it out," he said.

—2 KINGS 6:6–7

Today's Bible reading: 2 Kings 6:1–7

Today's verses record a mysterious little story about Elisha helping a man who had lost his edge—literally. His ax head had fallen off and sunk to the bottom of the Jordan River. Elisha asked a straightforward question: "Where did it fall?" And when he was shown the place, Elisha cut off a stick and threw it in the water. Next thing you know, the borrowed ax head was bobbing on the surface of the water. Elisha told the man to take back what he had lost. And he did.

Abruptly the story ends.

This simple story is a brilliant metaphor that goes beyond lessons in forestry. It gives you and me a basic action plan for the times when we sense we're losing our edge. Elisha's response to the young prophet gives us simple steps to take when we realize we're swinging hard at life but our effectiveness is slipping away. Or maybe has already sunk out of sight.

So what's the first step to getting your edge back?

It's realizing that you can't get your edge back by yourself.

🔁 RT If you cry out to God, asking Him to restore the passion you lost, He will answer—every single time. #GreaterBook

---

That's what the young prophet did. Rather than getting a pole to fish the ax head out or constructing a dam to dry up the river, he did the simplest and only thing he could do: he cried out. He realized that it was beyond his ability to restore what he had lost. His only hope was in the power of God to supernaturally give him back the ax head and relieve him from a debt he couldn't repay.

The next time you sense yourself getting spiritually dull, don't try to regain your momentum by doubling down on your self-effort. Instead, go to God. Even if you have to do it fifty times a day. He knows your weakness and He longs to give you strength. He doesn't want to put you through a series of lab tests to see whether you are appropriately sincere. He doesn't want you to wallow in regret. He just wants you to cry out—to call to Him. He wants to give you back your cutting edge. But He requires that you stop, get honest, and receive his grace.

I'll make a bold claim: if you cry out to God, asking Him to restore the passion you lost, He will answer—every single time.

Why wouldn't He? Do you think God wants you to stay stuck, frustrated, and ineffective?

It's hard to admit your ax head is lost. But there's power when you realize the ax head isn't gone forever—it's back at the place where you left it. And God will defy gravity in order to put it back within your grasp.

PRAYER FOCUS: Spend some time thinking about where you lost your spiritual edge. Then ask the Lord to help you get back to the place where you belong in Him.

God's Power, Our Strength

I pray that the eyes of your heart may be enlightened
in order that you may know the hope to which he has
called you, the riches of his glorious inheritance in his
holy people, and his incomparably great power for us
who believe.

—Ephesians 1:18–19

Today's Bible reading: Ephesians 1:3–23

Do you ever feel like you bounce from one weak moment to another? Life is clicking right along, you're gaining courage and momentum, then your kid comes home from school with a note from the principal's office. Or you think you'll finally start gaining ground on your debt, when an unexpected trip to the ER cuts your progress off at the knees. Or you think you've finally found the one relationship you've been dreaming of your whole life, when that person suddenly gets cold feet or a wandering eye and all those dreams shatter.

And you stare back at the reflection of yourself in the mirror and you see weakness. Loss. Rejection.

What you don't see is power.

How can we miss it—when our God has all the power in the world? It's because we've got to look at our situation with more than just human insight. Often we have to see, discern, and realize God's power not with a physical sense but with a deeper awareness. Scripture calls that sense "the eyes of your heart."

Paul's prayer for the church echoes the prayer of Elisha for his servant: "Open his eyes" (see 2 Kings 6:8–23). He prayed that the Ephesians would know how the power of God is accessible and available to them as ordinary, average, common believers. People like me. People like you.

Paul's prayer is not simply that Christians might know how powerful *God* is, although this is the starting place. Nor does he pray that God would *be* powerful, because He already is. Paul doesn't even pray that *we* would have more power, because in Christ we already have all the power we need for anything we are facing in our lives. Any circumstance. Every form of opposition we're ever going to encounter.

RT When I live by what God says, He opens my eyes to see what He sees. And He sees infinite power and potential in me. And in you. #GreaterBook

---

Instead, he prays that we would *know* for ourselves "that power" that "he exerted when he raised Christ"—and that this power would become a mighty strength in our lives.

Why does Paul pray this way? Because he knows the truth: it is possible for God to have all the power and yet for His people to live in total weakness.

Living in strength is all about taking hold of God's power and exerting it in our lives. But you can't put it to use if you don't know it's there. And you can't live it out if you're too focused on your weakness.

We don't live by what our physical eyes see. We live by what God sees and by what He says. When I live by what He says, He opens my eyes to see what He sees. And He sees infinite power and potential in me. And in you.

PRAYER FOCUS: Take Paul's prayer for the Ephesians, summarized in Ephesians 1:17–23, and turn it into a first-person ("I") prayer for yourself.

Grapes and Giants

They gave Moses this account: "We went into the land to which you sent us, and it does flow with milk and honey! Here is its fruit. But the people who live there are powerful, and the cities are fortified and very large."...

The men who had gone up with [Caleb] said, "We can't attack those people; they are stronger than we are.... All the people we saw there are of great size."

—Numbers 13:27–28, 31–32

Today's Bible reading: Numbers 13

The Israelites had finally reached the Promised Land. But it wasn't what everybody thought it would be. There was a reward, but there was also opposition. There were large grapes in abundance, but there were even bigger giants. So they came to the conclusion that this couldn't be what God was calling them to do. This couldn't be God's will, because, surely, God's will would be easier and safer than this.

We tend to think the same way. Many people consider opposition a sign that they must not be in the will of God. We think the

Promised Land is where the blessings—and *only* the blessings—are going to be. Being in God's will is where life is supposed to be easy. Therefore, if we experience a battle, opposition, or struggle, it must be a sign that we aren't in the right place. We must have mistaken the vision we thought God gave us.

But apparently a sign of God's will is not the ease with which you obtain it. Apparently the very sign that you've made it to the Promised Land is giants. Conflict. Opposition.

In other words, being in God's will doesn't guarantee a tension-free job. Or a conflict-free marriage. Or a trouble-free life. In fact, the very presence of tension, conflict, and trouble could be a sign that you're right where you need to be. Great struggles often indicate that much is at stake.

Despite all you've learned and dreamed about igniting God's vision for your life in the last four weeks, you might be thinking that you're not in God's will right now. The inner conflict is so severe, it must mean you're in the wrong place.

RT The presence of tension, conflict, and trouble could be a sign that you're right where you need to be. #GreaterBook

---

Not necessarily. It might mean that you're in exactly the right place, and you're closer to where God is taking you than you think you are. I doubt Satan is going to put up a fight to keep you from doing what you shouldn't be doing. What if you changed your perspective and saw what you're facing as a sign that you're exactly where God wants you to be, because giants are the welcome committee in the Promised Land?

That doesn't make it easy. But when you focus on the grapes instead of the giants, strength begins to rise.

The assurance of God's will isn't just the opposition you're facing. It's also the fact that, with God, you can actually overcome it. And the reward that you will get for sticking it out will ultimately outshine any opposition you are facing.

PRAYER FOCUS: Ask God to help you correctly interpret the opposition you're facing and give you the strength to battle your way through it.

Put Them Out

[Jesus] went in and said to them, "Why all this com-
motion and wailing? The child is not dead but asleep."
But they laughed at him.

   After he put them all out...

—Mark 5:39–40

Today's Bible reading: Mark 5:35–43

Not long after Elisha assumed Elijah's mantle, a bunch of juvenile
delinquents started taunting the baldheaded prophet: "Get out of
here, baldy!" (see 2 Kings 2:23–25). Not exactly a respectful recep-
tion for the man God had tapped to become His chief mouthpiece
for Israel.

There are always doubters for every dream. Naysayers for every
promise. Critics, mockers, and, yes, even haters.

As we saw yesterday, Caleb had them. Elisha had them. Jesus
had them.

And you and I have them. If we let them call the shots, we'll
miss so much of what God is saying to us.

So what do we do about them?

We can't let the voices of negativity keep us from going where

God is taking us. We have to determine to frustrate their doubt with our faith as much as they are attempting to frustrate our faith with their doubt.

If you're going to do what God has called you to do, you have to intentionally put out the people who subtract from your potential. That's what Jesus did to the people who laughed at His ability to raise the dead. He put them out of the room, out of His sight. Lesser faith has no place where God is about to do what's greater.

RT We can't let the voices of negativity keep us from going where God is taking us. #GreaterBook

---

Now, I know the concept of putting people out of your life may not sound very loving. But I'm not talking about drawing a circle around people and refusing to care about them. I'm talking about drawing some boundaries in your life and limiting what you receive from certain people. There's a big difference.

And it makes a big difference. If you listed the five people who have the most access to your life, I could predict with remarkable accuracy the course your life is going to take. Not because I'm Nostradamus. It's just simple logic. The people who have the most significant input into your life shape who you'll become and what you'll do.

Don't get me wrong. I'm not saying you need to abandon everybody who isn't going after greater things like you are. That's arrogance and the opposite of the attitude of Jesus, who was a friend of sinners (see Luke 7:34).

And I know you have people in your life—family and coworkers, for example—you can't get rid of. This isn't a license to change your last name or a command to quit your job. You'll just have to approach these relationships in a different way going forward.

The season when you are waking up to the greater call on your life is a powerful but fragile time. You'll face enough challenges ahead without taking along your own saboteurs.

Put them out.

PRAYER FOCUS: Think about the people who influence you the most. Then pray about how to restrict the voices of negativity that contradict what God is saying to you.

Finishing the Devil's Sermons

Jesus said to him, "Away from me, Satan! For it is written: 'Worship the Lord your God, and serve him only.' "

—Matthew 4:10

Today's Bible reading: Matthew 4:1–11

The same way that we have human opponents who try to stand in the way of where God is taking us, we have a supernatural adversary who is the enemy of God and the enemy of all that's greater. What do we do about opposition in the spiritual realm?

Lately I've seen a lot of power come to my personal life of faith when I finish the devil's sermons for him.

The concept of the devil preaching to you, much less you preaching back to him, may seem strange. But let me assure you, the devil is preaching to you all the time. He'll say things to you that contradict the Word of God. He'll say things that sound true on the surface but are designed to sabotage your life. He'll play on feelings of worthlessness, feelings of hopelessness right there in your brain to cause you to believe the lesser report rather than the greater report.

He did that to Jesus in the wilderness. Three times the devil came to the Son of God and tempted Him. If he had been successful in drawing Jesus away from the Father's will for Him, he would have aborted the greatest mission in history before it ever got started.

Yet, every time, Jesus prevailed. How did He do it?

Each time the devil preached a sermon, Jesus began his response with three simple words: "It is written."

🔁 RT Turn the devil's lies back on him with the truth of God's Word. #GreaterBook

---

Now, that's really powerful. The Word of God is the final word concerning any situation. It corrects every lie and half truth the devil puts out there to try to keep you from believing what God has said about you. You use the Word to finish the devil's sermon by mentally quoting scriptures and scriptural truths you've learned.

Here's an example. Let's say you're going through a trial and the devil says, "You'll never make it through."

Well, finish his sermon for him. Say to him: "Yeah, you're right, devil. On my own I'll never make it through. But I'm not on my own. I have a friend who sticks closer than a brother. Jesus said He would never leave me nor forsake me. He said He will be with me to the end of the age. So I'm going to make it through this trial with Him by my side." What you've just done is taken the evil that the Enemy has threatened you with and, as Genesis 50:20 says, turned it into the good that God intended.

You turn the devil's lies back on him with the truth of God's Word. In that way, your doubt can actually drive you closer to God rather than drive you away from God.

Finish the devil's sermon using God's Word. Then live by the truth instead of the lies. Don't let your enemy use doubt, temptation, or accusation to stop your progress in faith.

Remember, *greater* is He who is in you than he who is in the world.

PRAYER FOCUS: Pray for God to give you the ability to recognize the Enemy's schemes when he deploys them—and to effectively outflank his attack.

Detours to the Destination

The LORD blessed the latter part of Job's life more than the former part.... After this, Job lived a hundred and forty years; he saw his children and their children to the fourth generation. And so Job died, an old man and full of years.

—JOB 42:12, 16–17

Today's Bible reading: Job 42:7–17

When most people think of Job, the first picture that enters their minds is of a man marked by misery. That's natural, considering it's the theme of the first forty-one chapters in the book of Job. But it's also misguided because it doesn't take into account Job 42.

Job's story doesn't end on a note of misery. The final word on Job is not on his pain. His loss. His questioning. Or really anything resembling the forty-one chapters that precede the conclusion.

The final word on Job is an affirmation that he lived a full life. An affirmation that, despite appearances, God never for a second abandoned Job or changed His mind about Job's final destination.

The story of Job is more than a story about a guy who lost everything he cared about. It's also about a man who experienced restoration. A man who ended up dying the way he wanted. The way any of us would want. But not the way he or any of us would have planned.

He died surrounded by family, but it was a family that God had to recreate after he lost his first. He regained all of his possessions, and even had them doubled, but not before he had to lose everything he had worked his whole life for.

Job's final destination did not come without detours. Nor will ours. And it's the detours that have the chance to derail our progress more than anything else. Not because God can't see them coming or is incapable of handling them, but because we stick so closely to the path we think we're supposed to take to get to where God wants us to be.

RT The single greatest thing standing between you and God's plan for your life might be your notion of the road to get there. #GreaterBook

---

The single greatest thing standing between you and God's plan for your life might be your preconceived notion of the road you should take to get there. And it's a notion you have to hold very loosely.

You might lose your job. You may go through a period of marital unrest where it looks like everything is going to unravel. For a season, you may have to move to a place you hate. You may even have to face an unforeseen illness that threatens your life or the life of someone you love.

Whatever it is, detours are inevitable.

But just because God takes you on a detour, that doesn't mean He's changed His mind about your destination. The final word on your life is not going to be the detours you experience. It's going to be the destination God takes you to by way of those detours.

PRAYER FOCUS: Seek God's help to accept the detour signs He puts in your path—and to trust that He is still leading you toward a better end.

Great Calling, Great Cost

We who are alive are always being given over to death for Jesus' sake, so that his life may also be revealed in our mortal body.

—2 Corinthians 4:11

Today's Bible reading: 2 Corinthians 4

When we think about or discuss the apostle Paul, most of us focus on his incredible accomplishments. How he wrote two-thirds of the books of the New Testament. Took the gospel to the ends of the earth. Became the greatest missionary and one of the greatest preachers ever.

Sometimes we'll point out his suffering. But it's usually isolated. We use it to talk about pain and trials and how to get through them. Or how God's power is made perfect in our weakness. All of that is true, but I think we often miss a crucial point: Paul's accomplishments and his suffering went together. And there's a reason for that.

It's not because God had some kind of a secret vendetta against Paul. He had killed Christians, so why not make him drink a little of his own medicine while using him to spread the gospel? No.

As others have pointed out before, it's because, for Paul to be used greatly, he had to be wounded deeply. At the very beginning of Paul's Christian life, God declared, "I will show him how much he must suffer for my name" (Acts 9:16). He couldn't have become so great a servant if he hadn't been so great a sufferer.

RT God has to bruise you before He can use you.
#GreaterBook

The greater the calling, the greater the cost. Making a greater difference in the world means absorbing substantial pain. For the sake of God and for the sake of the people you're making a difference for.

That was true for Paul. And it will be true for you too.

Now, don't get me wrong, I'm not saying you've got stonings and floggings in your future. But I am saying that most of us want to do the kinds of things Paul did without having to go through the kinds of things Paul went through. And it doesn't work like that.

God has to bruise you before He can use you. So you'll be sensitive to His touch. So you won't have too much self-reliance in you. So you'll be able to relate to the people you're ministering to. So when everything is dark around you, the light within you will have a chance to shine.

If you really want to be used greatly by God, accept this now: You're going to be tried. You're going to be betrayed. You're going to suffer.

Like Paul, your great calling will exact a great cost. You'll be able to say, "We who are alive are always being given over to death for Jesus' sake, so that his life may also be revealed in our mortal body" (2 Corinthians 4:11).

But also like Paul, that won't be the final word for you. You'll be able to say, "Our light and momentary troubles are achieving for us an eternal glory that far outweighs them all" (verse 17).

PRAYER FOCUS: Think about the costs that you're already paying and that you might have to pay in the future for your faithfulness to God's vision. Ask Him to help you remain faithful through it all. And remind yourself that He's already paid the greatest price and made His all-sufficient grace available to you.

ABOUT THE AUTHORS

Steven Furtick is the *New York Times* best-selling author of *Sun Stand Still, Greater,* and *Crash the Chatterbox*. He is also the founder and lead pastor of Elevation Church, a multisite congregation based in Charlotte, North Carolina. He holds a master of divinity degree from Southern Baptist Theological Seminary. He and his wife, Holly, live in the Charlotte area with their three children, Elijah, Graham, and Abbey.

Eric Stanford is a writer and editor living in Colorado Springs, Colorado. Along with his wife, Elisa, he runs Edit Resource, LLC (editresource.com). They have two children: Eden and Elizabeth.

Dig deeper into God's vision for your life.

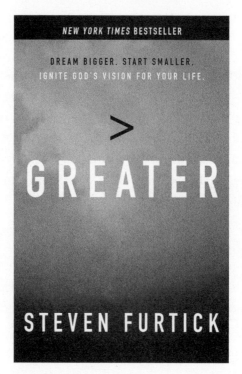

If you sense that you were meant for more but feel stuck where you are, *Greater* will give you the confidence to know that nothing is impossible with God, the clarity to see the next step He's calling you to take, and the courage to do anything He tells you to do.

Companion DVD also available!
Great for individual or group study.

Also from Steven Furtick

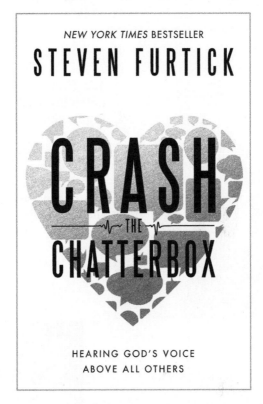

In *Crash the Chatterbox*, Pastor Steven Furtick focuses on four key areas in which negative thoughts are most debilitating: insecurity, fear, condemnation, and discouragement. With personal stories, inspiring examples, and practical strategies, you will learn how to silence the lies and embrace the freeing affirmation of God.

Companion DVD and participant's guide also available! Great for individual or group study.

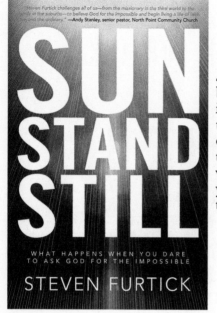
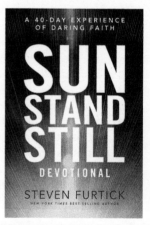